lonely planet

NOT-FOR-PARENTS

PARIS
Everything you ever
wanted
to know

Klay Lamprell

Planning our trip to Paris 2016. Cannot wait. Love, Grandma Susan

CONTENTS

IT'S A GREAT VIEW BUT I'M COLD AS STONE

HOP ON BOARD, TAKEOFF IS IN FIVE MINUTES...

WHY DOES EVERYONE CALL ME A DUMMY?

La Défense Grande Arche

Eiffel Tower

Dome des Invalides

Arc de Triomphe de l'Étoile

NOT-FOR-PARENTS

THIS IS NOT A GUIDEBOOK. And it is definitely Not-for-parents.

IT IS THE REAL, INSIDE STORY about one of the world's most famous cities—Paris. In this book you'll hear fascinating tales about **creepy stone gargoyles**, ghostly train stations, huge castles, and amazingly **pampered** pets.

Check out cool stories about stuffed animals, caves filled with **bones**, and the deadly **guillotine**. You'll find cyclists, junk collectors and musicians, and **snails** on the menu for dinner.

This book shows you a **PARIS** your parents probably don't even know about.

THAT SMILE

Is it a sad smile or a happy smile? That's the question people ask about *Mona Lisa*, the most famous painting in the world. The Italian artist Leonardo Da Vinci created this masterpiece over 500 years ago and brought it with him to France. Recent studies show that there are three different versions painted under the one that can be seen today. One version has her hands clutching the arms of the chair instead of in front of her.

SHE'S MY FAVORITE!

↑ *Mona Lisa*, c. 1503–5, Leonardo Da Vinci

A work of love
It took Da Vinci several years to make *Mona Lisa*. He used hair-thin layers of oil paint and glaze to create the smooth, misty effect that hides any brushstrokes. The painting was brighter—it has yellowed over time.

In 2005, a computer using emotion-recognition software decided that Mona is 83% happy!

Mona Lisa is so famous she receives her own fan letters each week!

WHEN IS MY LUNCH BREAK?...

I'M TAKING HER BACK TO ITALY.

MONA GOES MISSING

One night in 1911, after finishing work at the Louvre, Vincenzo Peruggia pulled *Mona Lisa* out of her frame and took her home! That was the last anyone saw of Mona for years. The crime remained unsolved until Peruggia was caught trying to sell her to a gallery in Italy. After that the work was guarded carefully.

Crowd in...
About six million people come to the Louvre every year to see *Mona Lisa*'s steady smile. She is kept safe in a box of bulletproof glass that has its own air-conditioning system.

Attention seeker
Opposite the *Mona Lisa*, which is simple and small, hangs the massive and very busy painting called *The Wedding at Cana* by Paolo Veronese. Measuring 22 x 33ft (6.8 x 9.9m), it's the biggest painting in the Louvre.

MOVE!

WHY WASN'T I INVITED?

↑ *The Wedding at Cana,*
1562–63, Paolo Veronese

WANT MORE?

The Louvre Museum—www.louvre.fr

UNE GLACE FOR BREAKFAST?

One in six Parisians owns a dog.

YOU CAN'T EXPECT ME TO WALK!

Dining with dogs
Dogs aren't welcome in many Paris parks, but almost all cafés and restaurants are happy to have dogs at their tables. Some even provide pooches with their own chairs!

Tote that terrier
Small dogs can travel on trains and buses as long as they are in a carry bag. On trains you pay half-fare if your dog is on a lead.

Dog delivery
Since not all taxis like to have animals in their cars, some companies in Paris provide special taxi services for dogs!

POOCHES IN PARIS

Dogs in France don't have to be vaccinated.

There are more than 300,000 dogs in Paris, possibly even more pooches than children! The French love their dogs so much they often take them to restaurants. Of course "what goes in must come out," so there's literally tons of doggy doo in Paris.

BEING A VEGETARIAN IS A MISSED STEAK

↑ *Le Carreau des Halles, 1880, Gilbert Victor Gabriel*

EWW!

BRING ME A BONE AND MAKE IT QUICK!

Curb your dog

Each year hundreds of people are admitted to hospital in Paris after slipping in dog poo! Signs on the pavements remind owners to make their dogs do their business in the gutter, not on sidewalks...

POSH POOCHES

When Parisian dog owners go away, their cherished canines can stay at Actuel Dogs hotel where they swim in the pool, run the doggy treadmill, and watch favorite DVDs. If you visit Paris with your pup, the grand Hôtel de Crillon offers "Dog de Crillon"—custom-sized beds, personalized collars, and delicious doggy delicacies.

WOOF!

WANT MORE?

The first pet cemetery opened in Paris in 1899.

THAT'S MR. EIFFEL TO YOU

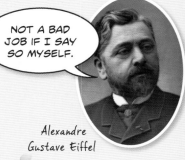

> NOT A BAD JOB IF I SAY SO MYSELF.

Alexandre Gustave Eiffel

Most people thought Alexandre Gustave Eiffel was an idiot when they saw the tower he designed for the 1889 World Fair. Parisians called it the "metal asparagus," but nobody was too bothered because it was supposed to be taken down after the fair. Of course, that was more than 120 years ago—these days it is the very symbol of Paris and considered a great work of art.

> PUFF!

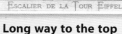

ESCALIER DE LA TOUR EIFFEL

ICE ON EIFFEL

Each winter an outdoor ice-skating rink is created between the steel latticework legs of the tower. Size-wise it's about as big as an average tennis court and holds up to 80 skaters at a time. At night colored lights and shapes are projected onto the ice.

> I DON'T HAVE A CLUE HOW TO SKATE, BUT WHO CARES?!

```
Mr. Eiffel also created
the internal frame of the
Statue of Liberty in 1885.
```

Long way to the top
There are around 700 steps up to the second level, which is 377ft (115m) high. From there elevators take you to the top which is 905ft (276m) high.

January 1888

April 1888

September 1888

A view fabuleux!

The tower stands 1063ft (324m) tall, about the same height as an 80-story building. It was the tallest man-made structure in the world for 41 years, and it's still the tallest structure in Paris!

Fast feat

The tower only took two years, two months, and five days to build. In total, 18,038 pieces of wrought iron had to be fastened together. Every seven years it has to be repainted, using 66 tons (60t) of paint!

TIMELINE

1887	Work starts on the Eiffel Tower.
1889	Building is completed.
1910	Theodor Wulf, a scientist and priest, finds more radiation at the top of the tower than at the bottom. This leads to the discovery of cosmic rays.
1912	Franz Reichelt, a tailor from Austria, straps on a homemade parachute and jumps from the first deck of the tower. He falls to his death.
1915	A radio transmitter on the tower receives the first radio signals ever sent across continents, from Arlington, Virginia in the United States.
1923	Alexandre Gustave Eiffel dies on December 27 in Paris.
1925 to 1934	A sign advertising the French car Citroën turns the tower into the world's biggest billboard.
1940	Nazi soldiers take over the tower, but French radio operators have already destroyed the equipment necessary for radio transmission.
1944	Hitler orders the military governor of Paris to demolish the city. The governor disobeys the order.
1956	Part of the tower is damaged by fire.
1984	Robert Moriarty flies a small plane through the arches of the tower.
1987	A.J. Hackett bungee jumps 360ft (110m) from the tower. He is arrested by the Paris police when he reaches the ground, but is released soon after.
1999	As the clock ticks over to the year 2000, flashing lights and fireworks erupt all over the tower.
2002	The Eiffel Tower records its 200 millionth visitor.
2004	An ice-skating rink opens for the first time on the first level.

WANT MORE?

Two-and-a-half million rivets hold the Eiffel Tower together. ✫ www.tour-eiffel.com

SQUARE OF THE GUILLOTINE

King Louis XV, who had no issues with low self-esteem, ordered that a huge square be built in Paris to show off a statue of himself on a horse. It took 11 years to build, and he called it Place Louis XV. But later the beheading of his son Louis XVI, along with his daughter-in-law Marie Antoinette and a few thousand other people, made a bit of a mess and gave the square a bad reputation—so the name was changed to Place de la Concorde.

Horror to harmony
The square was given a few different names before finally becoming Place de la Concorde. *Concorde* in French means harmony.

↓ *Execution of Louis XVI (1754–93), 21 January 1793*

> I SHOULD QUIT WHILE I'M A HEAD

Your royal nothingness
During the revolt against royalty known as the French Revolution, King Louis XVI was beheaded at the Place de la Concorde, then called Place Louis XV. By all accounts he met his fate with courage.

> SORRY SON, IT'S NOT WHAT I HAD IN MIND...

Louis XV

Cleopatra's Needle
To help distract visitors from the horror history of the square, a 3,300-year-old obelisk from Egypt was put in the center of Place de la Concorde in 1836. It is 75ft (23m) high.

Dr. Joseph-Ignace Guillotin

I'M AT THE CUTTING EDGE.

HEAD FIRST

In France before 1792 only the rich and powerful were lucky enough to have their heads chopped off. Others were hung, boiled, crucified, torn apart, or crushed! Then the law was changed, and anyone condemned to death would face the guillotine. The new device was named after Dr. Joseph-Ignace Guillotin, who had campaigned for the use of a reliable and fast-acting beheading machine.

Guillotin hated that the beheading machine was named after him.

Stain removal
It's thought that up to 40,000 people may have been beheaded in Place de la Concorde. The stone paving was often awash with blood! The square—which is actually shaped like an octagon—has long since been repaved.

WANT MORE?

The guillotine was abolished in France only in 1981! ✮ www.theguillotine.info

ARGHH!

ASTERIX THE GAUL

Asterix is the star of a famous comic strip set in ancient France, which was then called Gaul. The adventures of Asterix and his cartoon friends began over 50 years ago and now feature in books, movies, games, toys, and even a theme park near Paris! Asterix has millions of fans— not only French children, but kids and adults the world over.

Proud parents
Asterix was "born" in 1959 when illustrator Albert Uderzo (left) and writer René Goscinny (right) were asked to invent a cartoon for the French magazine *Pilote*.

I'M ASTERIX, I'M SMALL BUT FEARLESS.

I'M OBELIX, I EAT BOARS AND BEAT ROMANS.

Nothing boaring here
At Parc Asterix, amid the high-speed roller coasters, the swinging ship, the ride on rapids, and the bobsled track, they've created the village in Gaul where Asterix lives. You can even try the food he eats. Care for a wild boar burger?

(...T THEY WANT, ...DONYMUS. AND ...COULD BE A ...CK.)

RIGHT, O CENTURION.

HALT! WHAT DO YOU WANT?

WE WANT TO COME IN.

PLAFF!

CLAP! CLAP! CLAP! CLA...

NOW THIS IS WHAT I CALL ART.

Story time
Asterix, his friend Obelix, and the dog Idefix live in Gaul in 50 BC. They travel the world and meet Egyptians, Goths, and pirates on their quest to stop the Romans taking over their village.

The real deal
Asterix turned fifty in 2009. To celebrate, an exhibition showing original drawings and sketches was held inside a building in Paris that dates from Roman times.

Asterix comics have been translated into 107 languages!

R. GOSCINNY — ASTERIX — A. UDERZO

la Serpe d'or

Asterix in Paris
On the site where Paris now stands there was once an ancient Roman town called Lutetia. In the second Asterix book to be published back in 1962, Asterix and Obelix travel to Lutetia to buy a new sickle (*la serpe* in French) for their friend Getafix the druid. He needs it to cut his special herbs.

IF I CAN JUST FIND THE RECIPE FOR THE MAGIC POTION...

WANT MORE?

* **this is not an asterix, it's an asterisk ☆ Asterix Encyclopedia—www.asterix.com**

AXE HISTORIQUE

Forget axes and think axis—an imaginary line that cuts through the center of something solid. In this case the something solid is Paris and the imaginary line is a row of major monuments, buildings, and streets that run through the city from east to west. The line is called the Axe Historique, French for historical axis. Follow this line and the whole history of Paris is revealed.

3 Arc de Triomphe
Army general Napoléon Bonaparte took charge after the chaotic years of the French Revolution. The Arc de Triomphe was his idea. He wanted to honor his army with the kind of monument the ancient Romans used to build.

1 Ile de la Cité
The Parisii tribe settled along the River Seine about 2,500 years ago. Later, the Romans established a town called Lutetia on the south side of the river and on an island in the middle—Ile de la Cité.

> I'VE GOT HIGH HOPES FOR THIS VILLAGE.

2 The Louvre
The Romans abandoned Paris in the mid-5th century. For the next 1,400 years Paris (and France) was ruled over by a succession of kings and emperors. The Louvre, now one of the world's best-known art museums, was once a royal palace.

FIRST IN LINE

The Tuileries Palace, built in 1564, was originally the start of the Axe Historique. When the palace was burned down in 1871, l'Arc de Triomphe du Carousel, built by Napoléon in 1806, took up number one spot on the axis.

6 La Défense

Not long ago the axis was extended to the modern business district La Défense. The cubic Grande Arche is now the final monument in the lineup of the Axe Historique.

4 Metro station

Paris was one of the first cities to build an underground railway system. Line 1, which opened in 1900, follows the line of the Axe Historique with stops along the way.

IT'S THE NEW THING IN ARCHES...

"I AM FRANCE."

5 Avenue Charles de Gaulle

This avenue is named in honor of Charles de Gaulle. As a general he led the army at the end of World War II. As president, he reorganized the political system of France.

WANT MORE?

Paris history for beginners—www.forbeginners.info/paris/history

INSIDE OUT AND UPSIDE DOWN

The Pompidou Centre disgusted some people when it opened in 1977. This building has all its service pipes, ducts, and wires attached to the exterior—like a body with all its veins and nerves visible on the outside. Many thought it didn't belong in the middle of the city surrounded by elegant old buildings. Now it's one of the most popular places in Paris.

Pompiwho?
The actual name is the "Centre National d'Art et de Culture Georges Pompidou!" Pompidou was president of France. It was his idea to create a center for modern art in the heart of Paris.

The Centre is known locally as "Beaubourg."

WHAT'S WHAT

It's no secret how the building works—the pipes, tunnels, and ducts for the building's services and systems are attached to the outside and color-coded.

Air

Liquids

Electricity

Escalators and lifts

IS THAT A FACTORY?

Packing it in

Putting the escalators and other services on the outside means there is more space inside for the art museum, public library, cinema, performance halls, music institute, and shops!

Loved to bits

The Centre attracts about five times as many visitors as the designers expected. All those people wore out the building, and it had to be completely renovated within 20 years.

I'M THE FIREBIRD. I'M HOT!

I'M THE SERPENT. BITE ME!

FABULOUS FOUNTAIN

Next to the Pompidou Centre is a collection of 16 mechanical sculptures that move about and spurt water. The idea came from the music of composer Igor Stravinsky, which is why it's called Stravinsky Fountain.

WANT MORE?

Pompidou Centre—www.centrepompidou.fr

CITY OF LOVE

Paris is often called the most romantic city in the world, and it's easy to see why. It has been this way for centuries, with the French capital starring in countless poems, plays, books, and movies about love. More recently, a new tradition has sprung up where couples hang padlocks with their names on them on the Pont des Arts bridge, then throw the keys into the river.

YOU'VE SPELLED MY NAME WRONG!

Unlocking a mystery
Not everyone likes the love locks. When 2,000 of the padlocks disappeared from the bridge, some said the police cut them off, while others thought it was a single person envious of all the couples.

Love is in the air
Couples walk hand in hand along the Champs-Elysées, kiss by the River Seine, and sometimes even decide to get married by the Eiffel Tower.

EWW!

The French wedding cake is a tower of cream puffs!

The heart of Paris
The famous song *I Love Paris* by Cole Porter asks the question: "Why oh why do I love Paris?" He answers: "Because my love is here!"

The French for "I love you" is "Je t'aime."

Paris Opera ceiling by Marc Chagall

Love up above
The ceiling of the Paris Opera was painted by the artist Marc Chagall almost 50 years ago. Being Paris, the images include love-struck couples like Romeo and Juliet and Tristan and Isolde.

Read more about Rodin on page 74

I WONDER WHAT'S ON TV TONIGHT...

LANGUAGES OF LOVE

If you've ever wondered what a wall of love looks like, then look no further than this work by artist Frédéric Baron. Situated in the Square Jehan Rictus, it's made up of more than 600 tiles covered in "I Love You" written in 250 languages.

Lips locked in stone
No prizes for guessing what's going on in this marble statue by the French sculptor Auguste Rodin. And no prizes for guessing the work's name—it's *The Kiss* of course!

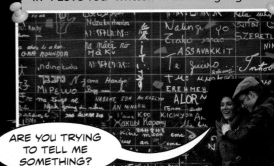

ARE YOU TRYING TO TELL ME SOMETHING?

WANT MORE?

Auguste Rodin, the sculptor of *The Kiss*, first made smaller versions in clay and bronze.

SNAILS ON THE MENU

Don't think of snails as those small, slow creatures that leave silvery trails as they slide, then slip back into their shells when scared. Think of them as dinner. The French are the biggest consumers of snails in the world. The best snails for eating are *escargots de Bourgogne* (Burgundy snails) and *petit gris* (small gray).

HELP!

Fancy a frog?
Frogs' legs used to be more common on the tables of Paris. But frogs in France are now protected, and imported frogs' legs are not as popular.

Slow preparation
Before eating snails you have to starve them for two weeks to get rid of their digestive muck. Not so hungry now?

HOW DO YOU LIKE TO BE COOKED?

IN BUTTER, PARSLEY, AND GARLIC.

The *croissant*

This crescent-shaped pastry is breakfast for many Parisians, and everyone has their favorite—more buttery, less flaky, a little salty, more chewy...

Mousse au chocolat

Mousse means foam, so egg whites beaten until they foam makes a mousse. Foam folded into melted chocolate is *mousse au chocolat*!

Stinky cheese

There are about 500 French cheeses, and the best are protected by law so that they can't be copied. French kids often finish a meal with a slice of stinky cheese.

The *baguette*

A symbol of France, the long, thin stick of bread known as a *baguette* varies in length, width, and weight according to baker and region. Old-school Paris *baguettes* were often 6.5ft (2m) long!

GALETTE DES ROIS

Also known as the king's cake, this is made each year for Epiphany on January 6. There is always *une fève* hidden inside—usually a tiny ceramic figurine. Whoever gets it in their slice is crowned with the gold paper crown that comes with the tart.

I'M KING OF THE WORLD!

Crêpes

Most nations have a version of flat, thin pancake—think of the Mexican *tortilla* and the Indian *dosa*. In France it's the *crêpe*!

WANT MORE?

In medieval times, snails were sometimes called wall-fish.

Going to ground
To get to the catacombs you have to go 65ft (20m) below the surface of the city, down a spiral staircase with 130 steps. At the entrance is a sign that reads: "Stop! Here is the empire of death."

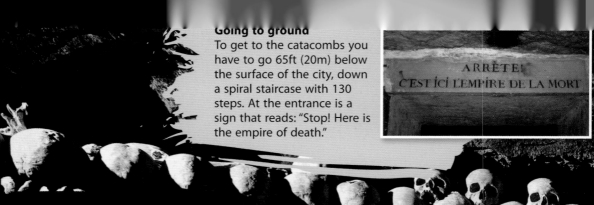

What else is down there?
The catacombs take up only a small part of the old mines beneath Paris. As well as 185 miles (300km) of mine tunnels, there are 1,200 miles (2,000km) of sewer tunnels, and 1,200 miles (200km) of railroad tracks!

LES CATACOMBES
1, Place Denfert-Rochereau →

I AIN'T GOT NOBODY TO CALL MY OWN.

DEM BONES

Under Paris are the catacombs—tunnels filled with the bones of six million people. They were put there around 200 years ago, moved from cemeteries that had become horribly overcrowded, causing bad smells, and the spread of disease. The bones were dug up and moved into old limestone mines underneath the city.

Bone art
Most of the bones have been carefully arranged, stacked in rows of arms, legs, and skulls. Some are arranged in artistic shapes like hearts and crosses. In some areas, though, bones are shoved in with little thought given to presentation.

Tourists and spies
Tours of the catacombs have been popular for about 150 years, though for a while during World War II the tunnels were used by members of the French Resistance as a hiding place from the Germans.

Carts to the catacombs
Priests blessed the bones as they were moved at night from the cemeteries to the catacombs in carts covered with black cloth. The work started in 1786 and took over 70 years to complete.

WANT MORE?

Catacombs of Paris Museum—www.catacombes-de-paris.fr

SWINGING SCIENCE

Giordano Bruno was burned alive for saying that Earth moved. Others after him thought the same, but no one could prove it. The French physicist Jean-Bernard-Léon Foucault found a way, and it made him very famous. After conducting the first practical demonstration of the rotation of Earth, Foucault went on to mess around with telescopes, mirrors, and the speed of light. He died a national hero, and his grave can be found in Paris's Montmartre Cemetery.

I WAS RIGHT!

Jean-Bernard-Léon Foucault

What a spinout!
A pendulum works best when there's a heavy weight at the end of the cable. Foucault used a 62-lb (28-kg), brass-coated lead cannonball.

SWINGING VOTE

A rod was attached to the pendulum to mark its movement in sand. At first it moved back and forth in a straight line, but then it appeared to swing counterclockwise. This proved Earth itself was moving!

Swing inside

Foucault hung his pendulum from inside the dome of the Panthéon. The Panthéon was first built as a church, but now it's just a grand building where many famous people are buried. An exact replica of Foucault's pendulum has been swinging inside since 1995.

The view from the Panthéon is one of the city's best.

All in good time

For centuries the steady swinging motion of a pendulum was the most accurate way to keep track of time. They were also an essential part of instruments used to record earthquakes.

YOU ARE GETTING VERY SLEEPY...

WANT MORE?

The Panthéon—www.pantheon.monuments-nationaux.fr/en

GUARDED BY GARGOYLES

So you want to scare away evil? Here's a plan. Decorate the outside of your building with some seriously hideous creatures—gargoyles. That's what they did with plenty of churches in Paris, including the massive Notre Dame. But despite its gargoyles, this cathedral is still haunted by the legend of *The Hunchback of Notre Dame*, the spooky story of a hunchbacked bell-ringer.

HAD A HUNCH YOU'D BE HERE.

Making an entrance
The Portal of the Last Judgement is a big doorway on the western side of the cathedral decorated with statues of Jesus and the apostles.

Local color
This is one of three stained-glass rose windows in the cathedral that have survived almost 800 years of fire, war, revolution—and some dodgy restoration work.

I MUST DO SOMETHING ABOUT MY POSTURE...

Middle ground
Point Zero, also called Kilometre Zero, is the official center of the city of Paris, and it's right in front of Notre Dame's main entrance.

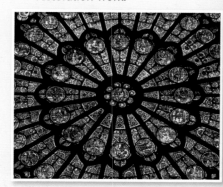

BOOK WITH BELLS ON

The Hunchback of Notre Dame is a famous novel by Victor Hugo. The main character is the cathedral's bell-ringer, Quasimodo. It has been made into many films, plays, and musicals, most of which are much more cheery than the original tragic story.

No competition but...
Notre Dame is the most popular tourist attraction in France, beating even the Eiffel Tower for total number of visitors.

ENOUGH WITH THE RINGING, I'M TRYING TO THINK!

WHAT A HUM-RINGER!

The big boy of Notre Dame's bells is the Emmanuel Bell, which tips the scales at over 28,000lb (13,000kg), not including its hammer, which weighs as much as a Citroën 2CV!

 =   OR  OR

1 x bus   3 x Indian elephants   2 x Tyrannosaurus Rex

WANT MORE?

Notre Dame Cathedral—www.cathedraledeparis.com

Hot property
In 2008, fire damaged the Cabinets of Curiosities, which are Deyrolle's most famous rooms, burning many of the animals. It's all restored now.

CURIOUS COLLECTION

It might look like a store, but Parisians say that Deyrolle is more of a museum than a simple taxidermy store. Taxidermy is the stuffing and mounting of animals for display, and at Deyrolle this has become an art form. This amazing place has been part of the Paris scene for more than 180 years, with its collection of stuffed birds and mammals, insects, shells, and much more.

OUCH!

GLUE

Taxidermy for beginners
Taxidermy is not for everyone! You have to remove the skin from the animal, wrap it around a model that is shaped like the creature, and then pop in some glass eyes.

Some of these animals can be rented for parties or movies.

Weird and wonderful
There are some bizarre items to be seen here, including an antelope's head on a dummy wearing an apron, ostrich eggs mounted on stands, and collages made of butterfly wings.

I'VE ALWAYS WANTED AN OFFICE WITH A VIEW.

WELL, THIS IS JUST EMBARRASSING!

RODENT'S RUIN

There's another Paris business that deals in dead animals. Julien Aurouze and Co. is a pest-control store with a window display of taxidermied rats. Some are displayed caught in traps or eating cheese, and others just hanging around.

WANT MORE?

Deyrolle once stuffed people's beloved pets.

KIDS IN CHAOS

In the early days of World War II, Germany invaded France. Paris was bombed, and hundreds of kids were killed. On November 11, 1940, high school students were the first to march in the streets in protest. Choosing that day was like sticking their tongues out at the Nazis. It was the anniversary of the day that France and other countries beat the Germans in the previous World War.

> I WAS ALSO A CARTOONIST!

Hard to resist
Jean Moulin was a famous member of the French Resistance. Many Paris schools and streets are named after him.

City without kids
In June 1940, Paris was evacuated before the German advance on the city. Many children were sent by their parents to live in rural areas with extended family.

Not happy, Hitler!
Not long after German troops claimed Paris in 1940, students protested at the Arc de Triomphe. The Germans shot at and arrested many of the protesters.

Opposing the occupiers
The French Resistance fought the Nazi occupation of France and worked against people who helped the Germans. They also helped people escape the country.

Daily rations during war
During the occupation, children weren't getting much to eat. The average height of children fell 2.7in (7cm) for boys and 4.3in (11cm) for girls.

DATES OF DESTINY

The German occupation of France lasted for just over four years. It started in June 1940, and residents suffered miserable conditions under Nazi rule until the city's liberation.

June 3, 1940
The German air force bombed Paris and killed more than 250 people, the majority of them women and children.

JUNE
S M T W T F S
1
2 3 4 5 6 7 8
9 10 11 12 13 14 15
16 17 18 19 20 21 22
23/30 24 25 26 27 28 29

August 24, 1944
After a six-day battle that started with an uprising by the French Resistance, German forces in Paris surrendered to Allied forces and the city was freed.

AUGUST
S M T W T F S
1 2 3 4 5
6 7 8 9 10 11 12
13 14 15 16 17 18 19
20 21 22 23 24 25 26
27 28 29 30 31

At home in Paris
The Nazis moved into hotels, police stations, and other public buildings in Paris, making use of local food and drink. Some of these buildings still bear bullet holes from the resistance.

SOME BUBBLES FOR YOUR TROUBLES HELMUT?

GO BACK TO BERLIN!

WANT MORE?

To save it from destruction, the government declared Paris open to the Germans.

CRUISE THE CAROUSELS

Back when it was important to practice wielding a sword or throwing a spear while riding your horse, you hopped onto a *carousel*, which was a basket or a wooden horse attached to a spinning central pole. Soldiers tested their accuracy in hitting a target as they spun around. Then someone got the idea that this could be a whole lot of fun, and the carousel, or merry-go-round, was born.

ONE DAY I'LL WIN THIS RACE.

WE CAN'T SEEM TO GET AWAY FROM EACH OTHER.

EVERYTHING SEEMS TO BE SPINNING!

PUFF!

Battle practice

The horsemen of the Middle East first invented the original carousel. The knights of the Crusades were impressed and brought the idea back to Europe.

DO-DO YOU LOVE A CAROUSEL RIDE?

Jardin de Plantes

SADDLE UP

The carousels of Paris have lots of cool mounts. There are pigs, elephants, zebra, and deer as well as extinct animals like dinosaurs and dodos, and imaginary animals like dragons and unicorns.

Parc de Bercy

Back in the day

The children of Paris have had the joy of merry-go-rounds in their parks and local squares for hundreds of years. Before steam engines were available to provide power, carousels were spun by hand.

WANT MORE?

National Carousel Association—www.nationalcarousel.org/european.html

ARC DE TOO LATE

The Arc de Triomphe could also be called the Arc de Too Late. Emperor Napoléon ordered an arch of triumph be built to commemorate his victories in battle. Trouble is, it was so big that it took 30 years to build. By that time Napoléon had been kicked out and the royals were back in power. Luckily King Louis-Philippe didn't hold a grudge—eventually he allowed the arch to be completed.

Eternal tribute
The Tomb of the Unknown Soldier under the arch is for all French soldiers killed in battle. The eternal flame has been burning since 1921.

IT'S SUPPOSED TO BE ALL ABOUT ME!

Symbol of bravery
The arch honors those who fought for France from the time of the French Revolution and the Napoleonic Wars.

Plane crazy
The arch is about 96ft (30m) high and 48ft (15m) wide—big enough to fly a plane through, as Charles Godefroy proved on August 7, 1919.

It's based on the Arch of Titus in Rome, but three times the size!

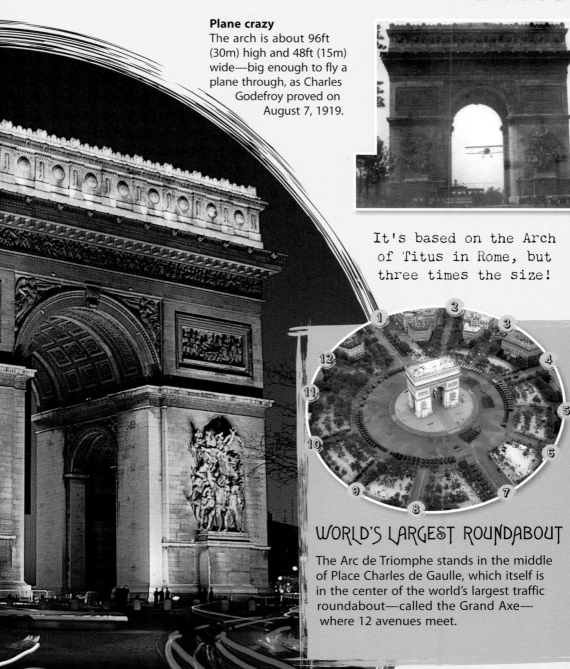

WORLD'S LARGEST ROUNDABOUT

The Arc de Triomphe stands in the middle of Place Charles de Gaulle, which itself is in the center of the world's largest traffic roundabout—called the Grand Axe— where 12 avenues meet.

WANT MORE?

Arc de Triomphe—www.arcdetriompheparis.com

SEWER TALK

I THINK I'VE FOUND THE JEWEL THIEF!

Rats!

In 1850, engineer Emmanuel Bruneseau was given the job of mapping the old sewer system before a new system could be built. He found lots of odd things down there including lost jewels, an orangutan skeleton, and thousands of rats.

Imagine if humans did their business on the streets, like dogs do. The people of Paris have to walk around through lots of pooch poo every day. The human stuff used to be dumped into the River Seine until it all got too smelly. That's when they got the idea of toilets up top and a sewer down below. Brilliant! Even more brilliant, they turned the sewers into a tourist attraction.

RUE
COGNACQ-JAY

Sewer traces street

The sewer tunnels almost exactly follow the layout of Paris streets. They even have wide sidewalks and signs that correspond with the names of the streets above.

All in a day's work
It's a tough job, but someone has to do it. Waders, masks, and headlamps are tools of the trade for *les égoutiers*— the highly regarded workers who keep the sewers of Paris running smoothly.

THEY FOUND A CROCODILE DOWN HERE ONCE!

Modernizing Paris
In the 1850s, engineer Eugène Belgrand designed new, large tunnels to carry waste and runoff water, and aqueducts to bring water from rivers into Paris homes.

SEWER SAFARI

In 1867, tours of the sewers were offered to the public, and they became a popular Paris tourist attraction. Visitors were taken through the sewers in wagons until 1920, when the wagons were replaced with a boat.

Wagon tours 1892–1920

Boat tours 1920–75

Today's tours
You can still explore a small area of the sewers, though these days the tour is on foot. The visit is designed around a museum called Musée des Egouts de Paris, which tells you everything you wanted and didn't want to know about the sewers. Yes, it smells!

WANT MORE?

Paris Sewers Museum—www.placesinfrance.com/musee_des_egouts.html

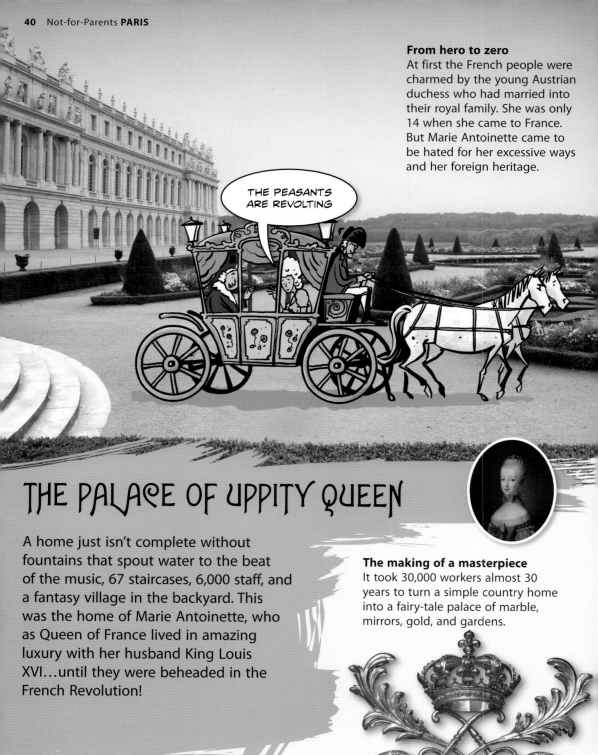

From hero to zero
At first the French people were charmed by the young Austrian duchess who had married into their royal family. She was only 14 when she came to France. But Marie Antoinette came to be hated for her excessive ways and her foreign heritage.

THE PEASANTS ARE REVOLTING

THE PALACE OF UPPITY QUEEN

A home just isn't complete without fountains that spout water to the beat of the music, 67 staircases, 6,000 staff, and a fantasy village in the backyard. This was the home of Marie Antoinette, who as Queen of France lived in amazing luxury with her husband King Louis XVI...until they were beheaded in the French Revolution!

The making of a masterpiece
It took 30,000 workers almost 30 years to turn a simple country home into a fairy-tale palace of marble, mirrors, gold, and gardens.

OH BOTHER! NOW I NEED THE BATHROOM.

Strike a pose

As queen of the country that set the trends for Europe, Marie Antoinette saw herself as a style guru. She went in for either over-the-top looks with exaggerated dresses and seriously big hair, or plain white outfits.

Playing peasant

A mini-village where Marie Antoinette would dress up and pretend to be a peasant was built for her in the palace grounds. It was known as the Queen's Hamlet. The peasants weren't amused.

Rude awakening

Unhappy with the way King Louis managed the country and with his wife's spending, the people forced the royal family out of Versailles. They lived under watch in the Tuileries Palace in Paris before being sentenced to death.

ROYAL FINALE

Marie Antoinette was in a dark, damp prison cell with her two children for over a year before being taken to her beheading through the streets in an open cart, her hair cut. Her last public words were an apology to her executioner for treading on his foot.

CELL-A VIE!

Marie Antoinette's prison cell exhibit

WANT MORE?

Palace of Versailles—http://en.chateauversailles.fr

SEINE AT YOUR SERVICE

Water, transport, and food—those are the basic reasons cities so often grow up around rivers. When the city is Paris and the river is the Seine, it's about more than basics—the history of the world is involved. The Seine has carried the body of Napoléon and the Statue of Liberty. It hosted the only Olympic obstacle and underwater swimming races. And its banks are on the list of World Heritage Sites in Europe.

The Seine splits Paris into Left (south) and Right (north) banks.

c. 1670

Floating services
As well as transporting goods and people, the Seine was a highway for boats selling fresh fish and offering domestic trades, like washing and mending clothing.

↑ *Fish Shop and Laundry Boat at the Quai de la Megisserie, c. 1670*

WHEN HE GOES UNDER, I'M OUTTA HERE!

SOLDIER ON FLOOD WATCH

How do you know when the Seine is flooding? When the water is lapping at the feet of the Zouave Soldier! This statue is attached to the Pont de l'Alma that crosses the river. When the Seine rises to the level of the soldier's feet, the sidewalks along the riverbanks are closed. In 1910, the waters reached his shoulders!

Salmon in the Seine

Before pollution messed up the water, there were plenty of fish in the Seine. Now the city has cleaned up its act a bit and the fish are back. They're unsafe to eat because of high chemical levels, but catch-and-release fishing for fun is catching on.

CATCH ME IF YOU CAN—BUT YOU CAN'T EAT ME!

Today

The modern river

As well as delivering basics like transport and some of the city's drinking water, the Seine supports one of the most important businesses in Paris—tourism. Glass-covered boats are an "in-seine" way to see the city!

WANT MORE?

River Seine—www.placesinfrance.com/river_seine.html

WHEELS AND BALLS

The biggest bicycle race in the world is the Tour de France, which goes for three weeks, covers thousands of miles, is watched by the whole world, and ends in Paris. But what is the best-loved sport in the city? Throwing a metal ball at a wooden ball! Two versions of this simple game are played—*boules* and *pétanque*.

I'VE GOT A FEELING I'M BEING FOLLOWED

ONLY THE RACE LEADER WEARS YELLOW.

Challenges ahead

The Tour de France has a different route each year, but it always takes teams of riders through towns and into rural areas, along flat and mountainous tracks, traveling inland and near the sea, enduring heat, cold, and wind.

Paris Start

Alps

Pyrenees

Winner takes it all

In the first Tour de France, many people cheated and fans beat up riders to stop them winning! Since then, drug cheating has scandalized the sport, but the high levels of skill and fitness still make it a thrill to ride in and to watch.

WHICH IS WHICH?

There is boules and there is pétanque. Boules is played by taking a few fast steps to power up and then tossing the ball. Pétanque is played from a standing position. The small wooden ball is called a *cochonnet,* which means piglet in French. It's also called a jack.

NOTE TO SELF:
NEXT TIME EAT LIGHT!

WAIT, WHOSE
TURN IS IT NOW?

From mock battles to boules
When the ancient Romans lived where Paris now stands, Arènes de Lutèce was a theater and arena where gladiators fought to the death. Now it's a boules court!

I REALLY MISS THE
BLOOD YOU KNOW

Arènes de Lutèce

For the love of the game
Wherever there is a park with a section of fine gravel, there are people playing boules and pétanque in Paris. Tournaments are often held alongside the artificial lake known as La Villette Basin and in the Luxembourg Gardens.

WANT
MORE?

The best mountain climber in the Tour de France wears a polka-dot shirt.

MASSIVE,

Castles were once homes for the royals and the rich, and these aristocrats ran their castles like mini-kingdoms—until the revolution, when everyone began to get a say. Your standard castle had to be tough enough to stop enemy attack, big enough to house lots of servants, and splendid enough to make people envious. Château de Chantilly near Paris is celebrated for its awesome gardens, grand stables, and sweet Chantilly cream that was created here by master chef François Vatel.

WHY AM I STUCK HERE IN THE KITCHEN?

Chantilly race
The landscaped grounds at Chantilly contain stables built to house 200 horses, a racetrack that is still used, and a museum devoted to horses.

MIGHTY, AND MAGNIFICENT

↑ *Banquet given on October 1, 1789*
Unknown artist

The gap between rich and poor
French nobility held huge, fancy dinners as a way of scoring points with royalty and one another. Just days after the banquet shown in this painting (left), ordinary women rioted because they could not afford bread for their families.

Chantilly lace

Chantilly cream

> NOW WHO'S GOING TO MAKE THE DESSERT?

> STOP!

FRANÇOIS VATEL

In 1671, 2,000 guests attended a dinner at Chantilly in honor of King Louis XIV. The master of the kitchen, François Vatel, was a super-perfectionist. When it seemed that the fish he had ordered was never going to arrive on time, Vatel couldn't stand the shame and ran himself through with a sword. The fishmongers showed up a short time later.

> MON DIEU! NO FISH— I CAN'T BEAR THE DISGRACE

WANT MORE?

Château de Chantilly—www.chateaudechantilly.com/en

ZOO ON THE MENU

When Prussians surrounded Paris and stopped food coming into the city, the people had no choice but to eat their animals! First went the horses. Around 70,000 became dinner. Then one by one beloved dogs, cats, and birds, and even pest creatures like mice and rats, were boiled and roasted. Castor and Pollux were more difficult to fit on the stove. They were elephants from the zoo. Other zoo animals went onto menus too. Luckily for animals in Paris zoos today, food is not hard to come by.

NO, I WOULDN'T CALL IT A CLASSIC MENU...

MENU

Pasta with dog sauce

Minced cat

Soup of horse

Elephant ice cream

Sausage of rats

↓ *Allegory of the Siege of Paris, 1870, Jean-Louis Ernest Meissonier*

SIEGE OF PARIS

In July 1870, France declared war on Prussia (now part of Germany). It wasn't a good move. Prussia walked all over the French army and kept on walking to Paris, where they encircled the city and settled in, intending to starve the Parisians into submission. The siege lasted for three months until the Prussians got sick of waiting and began shelling Paris until the people surrendered.

Pollux and Castor cooked
The elephants Castor and Pollux were popular attractions before the siege. They were bought by a butcher who sold the meat for good prices—especially the trunks, which were considered a delicacy.

Who's who at the zoo
The zoo at Jardin des Plantes was the first in Paris. It began when people were ordered to hand over their exotic pets. It now houses bison and anoas, birds and deer, Himalayan sheep, kangaroos, monkeys, antelope, and yaks. It has a baby animal section, a reptile house, and a microzoo for the study of insects.

WANT MORE?

The Museum of Natural History (including zoo)—www.mnhn.fr

WATER BY WALLACE

It's cool to be able to drink from a fountain instead of having to buy water in a bottle. In Paris, Richard Wallace is the guy we should thank for the free drink. He paid for over 100 public drinking fountains to be placed in different parts of the city. Well over a hundred years later they're still working—at least in the warmer months. In winter all the fountains are shut off so the pipes don't freeze up!

MY ARMS ARE ACHING!

IT'S MY GIFT AND I'M REALLY PUMPED!

Rich in spirit
Richard Wallace was a wealthy British art collector who lived in Paris. He wanted the fountains to be a gift of beauty and health to the city he loved.

IT'S A THEME PARK FOR FREE!

WET 'N' WILD

When it gets really hot in Paris and there's no swimming pool nearby, just jump in a fountain! As well as the fountains to drink from, there are plenty of big decorative fountains dotted around the city. Tourists and locals dangle their feet, splash in artistic jets of water, or just float about!

Keen inventor
There were four styles of Wallace fountains designed according to his guidelines. They had to be beautiful as well as practical. They had to be inexpensive to make and install. And they had to be placed where they could be easily seen, yet blend in.

The devil drink
Wallace thought that people might not drink as much alcohol if they had access to clean water. That's why one of the four statues on his fountains stands for sobriety, meaning being alcohol-free. The others represent kindness, charity, and simplicity.

NEXT TIME DON'T DRINK OUT OF THE FISHBOWL!

Wallace to the rescue
During the Siege of Paris 1870–71, the city's aqueducts were wrecked. Wallace's fountains made it possible for everyone to have water for free.

I HAD WATER ONCE. IT TASTED OF FISH.

WANT MORE?

The Wallace Collection—www.wallacecollection.org

THE PAINTINGS THAT

↓ *Starry Night,*
   1889, Vincent van Gogh

Postimpressionist
One of the most famous paintings next to *Mona Lisa* is *Starry Night* by Vincent van Gogh. Following the style of impressionists, he focused on light but he also put lots of emotion into his artworks.

THIS WORK IS GOING TO GIVE ME AN ART ATTACK!

→ *The Gleaners,*
   1889, Camille Pissarro

Magnified

WHAT IS IMPRESSIONISM?

Impressionists broke tradition by painting outdoors, capturing light and color at a particular time of day. Instead of blending colors on a palette, they used paint direct from the tube with short brushstrokes that put an accent on the effect of light.

CHANGED EVERYTHING

I AM FEELING A LITTLE BLUE TODAY.

For thousands of years, a good painter was one who created realistic images—even if they were imaginary. It was as though everything had been photographed. But about 150 years ago, artists in Paris stopped following the rules and began to blur the lines. The first stage of the new artistic style was called "impressionism." The second stage was called "postimpressionism." It changed the way people painted all over the world.

Train station then

Art gallery now

Museum in a train station
The Orsay train station, built for the Universal Exhibition of 1900, was later turned into the Musée d'Orsay, a popular museum that features art created between 1848 and 1914.

First impressionist
French painter Claude Monet was a founder of impressionism. The style features in paintings of his gardens in Giverny, with a collection of over 200 artworks entitled *Water Lilies*.

Monet's garden in Giverny

↑ *The Waterlily Pond with the Japanese Bridge*, 1899, Claude Monet

WANT MORE?

Musée d'Orsay—www.musee-orsay.fr/en/collections

THE PICKERS OF PARIS

IT'S A DIRTY JOB, BUT SOMEONE'S GOT TO DO IT.

Some people's junk is other people's treasure. That's what the *crocheteurs* or pickers of Paris understood over a hundred years ago. They picked through trash at night and by day set up stalls to sell the items they'd found. The stalls were called *marché aux puces* meaning market of fleas, because of the bugs in the secondhand goods. Now the markets are known just as The Fleas.

Night light
The pickers were also known as *pêcheurs de lune*—meaning moon fishermen—because the moon was their main source of light as they fished through the piles of trash.

GOTTA JUMP ON A BARGAIN!

BEST FIND EVER? A REAL GOLD FISH.

Back in the day
The pickers weren't allowed to sell their stuff inside the city walls, so they set up in areas just outside of Paris. In 1885, the neighborhood of Saint Ouen paved specific streets for the sellers to work in, and The Fleas became official!

NO, I PROBABLY WOULDN'T SUIT EVERY HOME...

I CAN'T KEEP THIS POSE FOREVER. BUY ME!

Market mile

The Fleas are now a bunch of different markets, each with hundreds of open and covered stalls. It's big—like ten soccer fields big—and over 100,000 people hang out there each weekend!

Dig in

With its rich history and years of royal splurge, Paris is an endless source of treasure-trash, from clothes to clocks, stamps to statues. Some sellers clean up their wares and display them with care. Others shove stuff in a box and let buyers go for it!

There's an app for that-- Keys to the Fleas!

WANT MORE?

Flea Markets official site—www.parispuces.com/en

Many Paris street names tell a story. With some, the story is told in the name changes through history. With others, the name itself tells a story, like the Rue du Chat-qui-Pêche, which means Street of the Cat Who Fishes. Can you guess what the story might be?

Just 6ft (1.8m) wide...

STREETS THAT

Rue de la Paix

The modest (not) emperor Napoléon knocked down a convent and other buildings in 1806 to create an avenue of elegance that he called— you guessed it—Rue Napoléon! After the Napoleonic wars it became Rue de la Paix— Street of the Peace. It's known for luxury stores, and for being the most expensive street on the French Monopoly board.

Rue du Chat-qui-Pêche
This narrow street used to end at the River Seine. During floods, the cellars of houses in the street filled with water. The story goes that one smart pussycat used to catch fish in the cellar of his house by sweeping his paw through the floodwaters. That's why it's called the Street of the Cat Who Fishes! It's the narrowest street in Paris.

2ᵉ Arrᵗ
RUE DES DEGRES

Rue des Degres
The shortest street in Paris, Rue des Degres or Street of Degrees, is just over 10ft (3m) wide and 16ft (5m) long! Basically it's a stairway with 14 steps.

TELL A STORY

16ᵉ Arrᵗ
AVENUE DE NEW YORK

IT'S MINE!!!

I'M NOT HAPPY...

Avenue de New York
It was first named after a French general, Jean Louis Debilly, who died in 1806. In 1918, the name was changed to Avenue de Tokio. It was a way for France to say "merci" to Japan for being an ally in World War I. Things changed again after World War II. This time Japan was an enemy of France. Avenue de Tokio became Avenue de New York, to thank the USA for helping to kick out the Germans!

WANT MORE?

Searchable street map of Paris—www.parismapped.com

GHOST STATIONS OF THE METRO

There are four ghost stations under Paris—train stations that were once part of the Metro system but are no longer in use. These stations closed down during World War II and never reopened. Besides the fact that they're covered in graffiti, they remain intact, and there are old prewar advertisements on the walls, selling long-forgotten products. The only visitors these days are the homeless and tour groups.

Signs of the times
The first "Métropolitain" signs were hung on iron supports that looked like plants. Next came "Métro" signs with round lamps on top, and finally the design of an "M" in a circle.

I'VE BEEN WAITING 50 YEARS FOR MY TRAIN!

ALL WE GET HERE ARE GHOST TRAINS.

Abandoned Saint-Martin
Saint-Martin is the city's largest ghost station. And the trains won't be back any time soon—the tracks are cemented over!

Snakes on a train

In 1938, this boa constrictor was discovered riding the Metro unaccompanied and without a ticket. The *pompiers* (firefighters) caught it and *les flics* (the cops) took care of the rest.

THIS WAS A LENGTHY INVESTIGATION!

VEINS OF THE CITY

The Paris Metro now carries around four million passengers every day in one of the densest underground networks in the world. Without it, Paris would grind to a halt.

Making tracks

The first line of the Metro opened in 1900 during the World Fair, with wooden carriages that are now only found in museums.

Thoroughly modern Metro

The system now has 16 lines, some of which have been operating for more than 100 years. Others have been completely revamped to become fully automatic, driverless services.

Railway sleepers

Saint-Martin is now a place where homeless people can have something to eat then spend the night out of the cold and rain.

Paris or busk!

You need to pass an audition to obtain one of about 350 official licenses that allows you to play music in the Paris Metro system.

WANT MORE?

The ghost stations were used as bomb shelters during World War II.

THE MELTING POT OF PARIS

After World War II, France was in a mess. Lots of people had left or died during the war and to put itself back together again, France needed workers. So it asked people from Africa and Asia to come to France to live and work. They did, bringing their clothing, food, music, art, and religions. Modern Paris is one big multicultural melting pot!

West Africa
Senegal in West Africa used to be a French colony. Senegalese troops fought for France in World War II, and today thousands of Senegalese call Paris home.

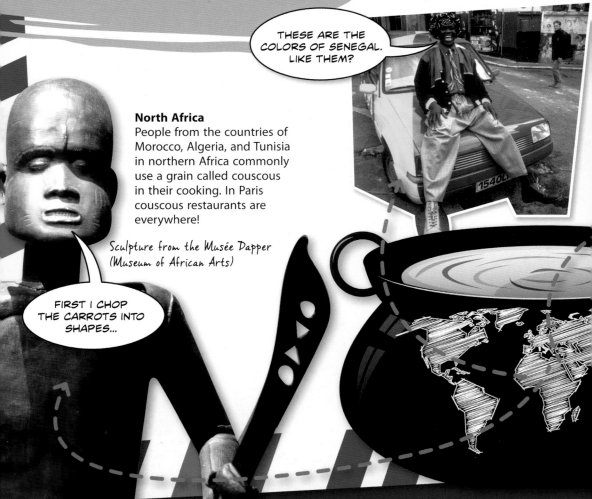

THESE ARE THE COLORS OF SENEGAL. LIKE THEM?

North Africa
People from the countries of Morocco, Algeria, and Tunisia in northern Africa commonly use a grain called couscous in their cooking. In Paris couscous restaurants are everywhere!

Sculpture from the Musée Dapper (Museum of African Arts)

FIRST I CHOP THE CARROTS INTO SHAPES...

IT'S ONE BIG PARTY, DUDE!

Arabic

Many immigrants in Paris are from Arabic-speaking countries. The Arab World Institute is decorated with cool geometric patterns. Even cooler, the patterns work like the aperture of a camera lens—opening and closing to control the amount of sunlight that gets inside.

THE WALLS HAVE EYES!

Little Jaffna

Ganesha, the elephant-headed Hindu God, gets his own festival each year in Little Jaffna. It's a part of Paris where thousands of people from Sri Lanka have settled.

Asiatown

The biggest of the two Chinatowns in Paris should really be called Asiatown because it has lots of people from other parts of Asia, like Vietnam, Laos, and Cambodia. Many Asians first came to Paris in the 1970s to escape wars and cruel governments.

CHECK OUT OUR MOVES!

WANT MORE?

Even in the Middle Ages, people from other countries flocked to live in Paris.

SHOP THE CHAMPS-ELYSÉES

She's grown fruit and vegetables, been nibbled on by sheep and pigs, and had army tanks roll over her. She's been lengthened, widened, built on, lit up, and put in costume for special events. She's a road to drive down, a path to walk along, and a street to shop on. So how do you say her name? Say shawn-zay-lee-zay.

Champs-Elysées means Elysian Fields--the resting place for souls of heroes in ancient Greece.

WE ARE FABULOUS, OUI?

Place Charles de Gaulle

Celebration street
The Avenue des Champs-Elysées is the place Parisians head to when there's something to celebrate, like the end of the Tour de France bike race, midnight on New Year's Eve, and Bastille Day, the French national birthday.

Auto alley
Being one of the most famous avenues in the world, the Champs-Elysées is home to some of the most famous brands in the world—clothing, shoes, jewelry, accessories, and even cars!

Café culture
The café-brasserie lineup on the Champs-Elysées includes Le Fouquet's, which has been running so long—since 1899—that it's been listed as a historic monument. The French film awards ceremony, the Césars, ends with dinner here.

Avenue des Champs-Elysées

Place de la Concorde

WANT MORE?

Champs-Elysées official website—www.champselysees.org

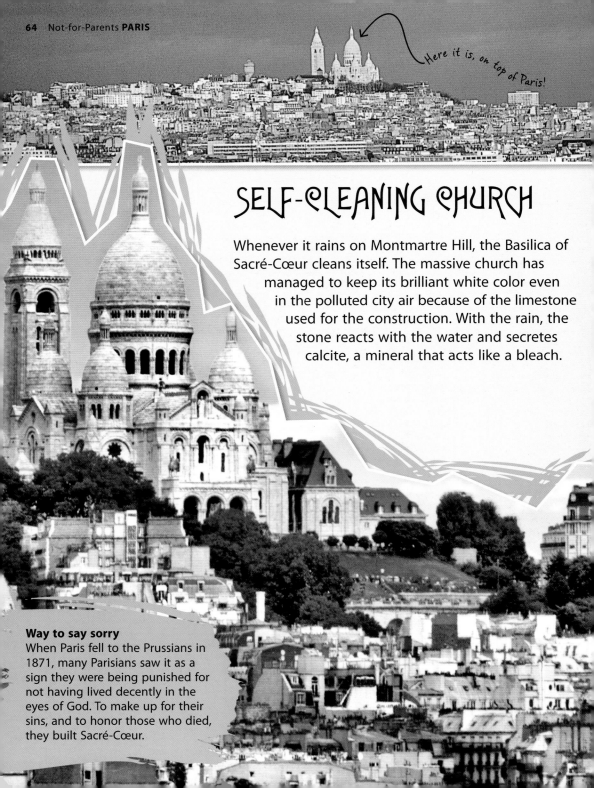

Here it is, on top of Paris!

SELF-CLEANING CHURCH

Whenever it rains on Montmartre Hill, the Basilica of Sacré-Cœur cleans itself. The massive church has managed to keep its brilliant white color even in the polluted city air because of the limestone used for the construction. With the rain, the stone reacts with the water and secretes calcite, a mineral that acts like a bleach.

Way to say sorry
When Paris fell to the Prussians in 1871, many Parisians saw it as a sign they were being punished for not having lived decently in the eyes of God. To make up for their sins, and to honor those who died, they built Sacré-Cœur.

Perched on a hill, Sacré-Cœur looks out over the city.

IT'S ONLY A FLESH WOUND!

GASP!

HEADSTRONG!

In the 3rd century, when Christians were being persecuted, the bishop of Paris, named Denis, was beheaded. The story goes that he picked up his head and walked many miles to the north, preaching all the way. He finally died at the spot where Sacré-Cœur now stands.

Sacré-Cœur means Sacred Heart.

GUARDIAN STATUES

At the entrance to Sacré-Cœur are two bronze statues of French saints. St. Joan of Arc led the French to victory in war, while King Louis IX was sainted for being a kind and fair ruler.

St. Joan of Arc

King St. Louis IX

WANT MORE?

Official website—www.sacre-coeur-montmartre.com

FOUR LADY LIBERTIES

The Statue of Liberty in the USA that towers over the entrance to New York Harbor was designed and built in Paris, then shipped to its new home in pieces! Paris has three of its own Lady Liberties— two are models used by the sculptor Bartholdi in designing the statue, and the other is a thank-you gift from the USA to France.

IT'S ALWAYS ALL ABOUT HER...

Frédéric Bartholdi

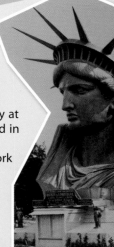

Luxembourg Gardens

LADIES IN PARIS

I THOUGHT SHE WAS MUCH BIGGER!

The Statue of Liberty in the Luxembourg Gardens is Bartholdi's bronze model. His plaster model is in the Musée des Arts et Métiers. Then there's the Lady given by the Americans to the French. She lives next to the Pont de Grenelle, south of the Eiffel Tower. At 33ft (10m) high, she's a mini-me. The real deal is 305ft (93m) tall!

Musée des Arts et Métiers

South of Eiffel Tower

Flame of Liberty
The torch held by Lady Liberty stands for open-mindedness and keeping the flame of freedom alive. A life-size copy of the torch sits above the entrance to the Pont de l'Alma tunnel near the Champs-Elysées.

Way ahead
Bartholdi began work on the Lady in 1870. Her head was put on display at the World Fair held in Paris in 1878. She opened in New York eight years later.

Making of a lady
Alexandre Eiffel, who created the Eiffel Tower, built the internal frame for Lady Liberty. She was sculpted in copper by Frédéric Bartholdi and then shipped from France in 350 pieces.

SCENIC CEMETERY

The biggest cemetery in Paris—and one of the most visited cemeteries in the world—is Père Lachaise. Under its humble headstones and inside its towering tombs are famous writers, singers, poets, and lovers. They attract hundreds of visitors each day, and it's rumored that secret societies meet there at night!

Burial space

In the late 1700s Paris had a problem with smelly, overcrowded graveyards. The solution was to move millions of bodies to the catacombs (see pages 24–25) and open new cemeteries beyond the city center. Père Lachaise was opened in 1804.

Jim Morrison

Jim Morrison, lead singer of the sixties band The Doors, lived hard and died young in Paris. His grave is the most popular spot in Père Lachaise. It's guarded and fenced off now because Morrison fans were making a terrible mess and writing bad poems on all the nearby gravestones.

THE LIZARD KING IS DEAD DUDE. WHAT A BUMMER.

GET EMOTIONAL FROM OVER THERE!

Jim Morrison

WOUF! WOUF!

Oscar Wilde

It's tradition for visitors to kiss the tomb of witty Irish writer Oscar Wilde, who died in Paris in 1900. His motto in life: "Be yourself. Everyone else is already taken."

I CAN RESIST EVERYTHING EXCEPT TEMPTATION!

RIN TIN TIN—MOVIE STAR

Along with all the famous people buried in Paris, there are also famous animals! Rin Tin Tin moved to Hollywood from France as a puppy and found fame and fortune. His body was returned to Paris and buried in the Cimetière des Chiens, the cemetery for dogs.

WANT MORE?

Père Lachaise Cemetery—www.pere-lachaise.com

SHOCK CHIC

The leading lady of early Paris fashion, Coco Chanel, got rid of the bone corset that made it hard to move. She put women in pants and told them to start thinking for themselves. Outrageous! Now a whole new range of outrageous turns up on the catwalks of Paris every year. No one is expected to actually wear the clothes, but they do influence trends all over the world.

"THE MOST COURAGEOUS ACT IS TO THINK FOR YOURSELF."

Gabrielle "Coco" Chanel

FASHION VICTIMS

Chanel's designs were all about giving women their independence through ease of movement. The corset was the opposite. Pulled in tight to give a false shape, it made even breathing difficult.

Chanel classic
Coco Chanel worked hard, and she wanted all women to be able to work hard, too, so she created a women's suit that is now considered a classic Chanel look.

I CAN'T BREATHE, LET ALONE TALK!

Length and layers
Before Chanel, women wore not only a corset and long fancy dress, but a chemise, drawers, and layers of petticoats, all made by hand. Only the very rich could afford to look good.

Chanel

Start of 1900s

Design first, sketch later
It's been said that Chanel didn't draw sketches of her designs—instead she created a look on a model, then an artist put the image on paper.

070

Fashion club
There are two Paris high-fashion shows a year. With a starting price of $30,000 per outfit, only around 500 people in the world actually buy the clothes from the Paris catwalks!

Jean Paul Gaultier

Fashion rules
The most exclusive clothing in the world is known as *haute couture* (high sewing). The term is legally protected in France.

Pierre Cardin

Givenchy

IT'S ALL ABOUT THE BAG THE CLOTHES COME IN!

Skirts for men
Well, there was a time when no one believed women would wear trousers and shorts. Perhaps what we see on the catwalk now will become everyday clothing for men!

WANT MORE?

In 1910, Coco Chanel kicked off her fashion career by opening a hat store.

MOVE HER TO THE LOUVRE

The very old and very famous statue of Venus—the goddess of love and beauty born from the foam of the sea—was lost for a long time. One day a peasant trawling for treasures in the rubble of an ancient city found Venus. She was in a sorry state, broken into pieces and missing her arms. She was moved to the Louvre in Paris—the world's most visited art museum—where she was put back together.

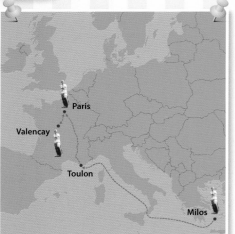

Journey to Paris
Venus was found in 1820 in the ruins of an ancient city on the island of Milos, which is why she is called Venus of Milo. She was put onto a French ship and delivered to King Louis XVIII, who gave her to the Louvre.

Venus, *Mona Lisa*, and more...
It's been said that it would take at least nine months to take a look at every work of art in the Louvre— there are over 35,000 artworks to see!

Originally Venus was painted and wore jewelry.

HANDS-OFF

Venus was found in pieces—big bits of body and legs and smaller bits of a hand and arm. When the Louvre put her back together, they weren't sure that the hand and arm were original so they didn't put them on. They've worked out that the missing arm would have held an apple.

Wartime security
When World War II hit Europe, the Louvre was worried Venus might be smashed up or stolen, so they sent her for a vacation in the countryside until Paris was safe again.

The French had to fight the Turkish for possession of the statue.

WANT MORE?

Musée du Louvre—www.louvre.fr

PLASTER OF PARIS

Have you ever drawn with chalk, hit a *piñata*, or signed the cast on a friend's broken arm? Then you've had contact with the same material used by the world's most famous sculptors. Plaster of Paris is the name given to a mixture of water and a powdered rock called gypsum. There used to be a lot of gypsum in the hills of Paris, so that's what sculptors like Auguste Rodin used—and that's where the name Plaster of Paris came from.

Auguste Rodin

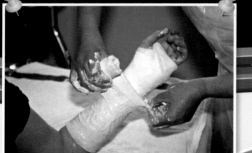

Medically speaking
Bandages coated in plaster of Paris that harden after they're applied are one way to create a healing shell around a broken limb. These days fiberglass is often used.

NEXT BEST THING TO THINKING—LOOKING LIKE YOU'RE THINKING!

The Thinkers
Rodin created a small plaster version of his most famous piece, *The Thinker*, before sculpting a bigger version in bronze and marble. It was so popular he had more cast, and people have been copying it ever since.

I THOUGHT I MIGHT MAKE THE TOE BIGGER...

JUST DO IT LIKE I TOLD YOU!

Rodin the boss
The process of creating a plaster cast and turning it into a bronze sculpture is complex. Like other sculptors, Rodin hired artists to do the work.

SAFETY IN PLASTER

The museum of architecture in Paris, called Cité de l'Architecture et du Patrimoine, holds a large collection of perfect plaster casts of historic monuments, sculptures, and buildings, so that if the real thing is damaged they can re-create it accurately!

WANT MORE?

In the 1700s, the King of France ordered all wooden houses to be covered with plaster.

FIRST BRIDGE ACROSS THE SEINE

Paris is a city divided by the River Seine but connected by bridges. Paris bridges used to have shops and houses built on them and were a center of city life and entertainment. The first bridge across the Seine was the old Pont Notre-Dame, which connected the river island of Ile de la Cité—the site of the grand Notre Dame Cathedral—to the main part of the city. In 1499, the bridge collapsed under the weight of 60 houses!

Jouster

Top security
Around Paris are many *mascarons*—heads or just faces that guard buildings and bridges from bad spirits. On Pont Notre-Dame there is a carving of Zeus, the god of all gods.

A bridge remodeled
The new Pont Notre-Dame was built in 1853, and was nicknamed "devil's bridge" because its five small spans made it dangerous for boats to pass, causing many accidents. In 1919, a single span replaced the middle three.

↓ *Jousting of the mariners between the Pont Notre-Dame and the Pont-au-Change, 1756, Nicolas Raguenet*

Spectators

Bridge structure

AT LEAST I MAKE A SPECTACULAR LOSER!

Spectator sport

From the 13th century the sport of water jousting was played by fishermen and boatmen on the River Seine for the entertainment of both the lower classes and nobility, who watched from boats nearby and from Pont Notre-Dame.

TOURNAMENTS TODAY

Although it has been played for centuries, it was just 50 years ago that water jousting became an official sport in France. The opponents try to push each other into the water using lances. (It hasn't taken off as a winter sport.)

The French word for bridge is "pont."

LONG LIVE THE BLUES...

WANT MORE?

In Paris, there are 37 bridges that span the Seine.

OW!

I'LL DO HIM A NICE HAT...

I'M KNITTING HIM A NICE SCARF

Execute the king
They beheaded King Louis XVI at the Place de la Concorde. He had been stripped of all titles, so he died as Louis Capet.

Weapon up!
First the crowd headed to Les Invalides, where the army kept its weapons. They stole over 30,000 guns, but still needed gunpowder.

WHAT YOU GET FOR BEING GREEDY

The people of Paris had enough of greedy rulers. King Louis XVI, his snobby wife Marie Antoinette, and their big-headed friends were pigging out on delicious food, wearing cool clothes, and having a stack of fun while most people hardly had enough money to feed their children. The crowds got really worked up one day and decided to do something about it. That was the start of the French Revolution.

WE CAN'T FIGHT WITH BAGUETTES!

Get rid of the rest
They put Queen Marie Antoinette and 3,000 other people into a prison called La Conciergerie and executed them a few at a time.

Bastille Day
Next they headed to the Bastille prison where they took all the gunpowder and supplies they needed and freed prisoners.

4ᵐᵉ ARRᵗ

PLACE DE LA BASTILLE

WANT MORE?

LITTLE MAN, BIG EMPIRE

He had Italian parents, spoke French with a Corsican accent, and in his early days was so small and thin that he was nicknamed "Little Corporal." But being different didn't bother Napoléon Bonaparte. He became Emperor of France, overhauled the legal system, and took over much of Europe. Though eventually he was thrown out of his beloved country and imprisoned on a remote island, Napoléon had changed France forever.

HIT ME WITH A CANNONBALL AND I'LL BE NAPOLEON BLOWNAPART

It's all about me...
The plans for Napoléon's coronation as emperor were as strategic as his planning for battle, and as ambitious. He insisted on maximum bling at the grandest cathedral in Paris—Notre Dame.

Curious conqueror
Napoléon headed to Egypt to expand France's empire. He was hungry for power but he was also intrigued by the Middle East. He brought scientists to study and write about the area.

BOOM!!!

I CAN'T GET ANY LOWER!

Winning ways

As a young general, Napoléon put down a rebellion on the streets of Paris with expertly placed cannons firing loosely packed balls of iron. This won him fame and a big promotion.

OOPS—SORRY BIRDIE!

1769	Born in Corsica, which is part of France but lies near Italy.
1785	Graduates from military college as an officer.
1789	The king is deposed and the French Revolution begins.
1796	Becomes commander of the French army in Italy.
1796	Marries Joséphine de Beauharnais, a widow with two children.
1798	Wages war against Egypt.
1799	Helps to overthrow the French government.
1804	Proclaims himself Emperor.
1808	Wages war against Spain.
1809	Divorces Joséphine because she hasn't given him any children.
1810	Marries Marie-Louise, Archduchess of Austria.
1812	Fails in war against Russia. Further failures follow.
1814	Gives up his title as Paris is taken by anti-French forces.
1814	Sent to live on the island of Elba, off the coast of Italy.
1815	Brought back to France to fight the British and Prussians, but fails.
1815	Surrenders to the British, who send him to live out his days on Saint Helena, one of the most isolated islands on Earth.
1821	Dies.

I DEMAND A STEPLADDER!

Safely tucked away...

The body of Napoléon is inside a coffin that's inside five other coffins that are inside a tomb! The tomb is kept in a chapel that is part of a museum called Les Invalides (see pages 92–93).

WANT MORE?

Napoléon started military training when he was nine. ☆ www.napoleon.org

The scandal of the cancan
Music halls became known for the cancan, a dance that was considered a scandal when it was first invented. Women in a row would kick so high you could see the long pants they wore under their skirts. The costumes these days are even more revealing!

CANCAN DANCE...

On the hill of Montmartre overlooking Paris is a dance hall that's been going since 1889. The area was once covered in vineyards, and dotted with windmills for making flour. People came to the area for the wine and stayed in country inns that competed for guests by putting on dance shows called "cabarets." These became dance halls. Today, only the Moulin Rouge ("red mill") is left.

THE ART OF DANCE

Henri Toulouse-Lautrec, one of the legendary artists living in Montmartre in the late 1800s, painted posters of the Moulin Rouge. His subjects were often the dancers, like La Goulue (her real name was Louise Weber), who was known for a heart sewn on to the seat of her pants—outrageous!

In the 1700s there were over 130 cabarets in Montmartre!

Spectacular

The Moulin Rouge is now a hugely popular tourist spot with nightly performances of the cancan by dancers in seriously over-the-top costumes (think feathers and fake jewels). There are also acts by acrobats, magicians, and clowns.

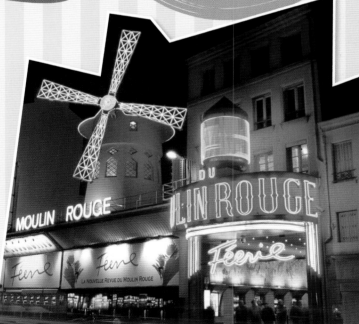

WANT MORE?

How to dance the cancan—www.ehow.com/how_2064493

PARIS ROCKS!

Jazz it up
The sound of jazz first blew into Paris from the USA in the 1920s. The French made jazz their own by adding different instruments, like violin and guitar.

The beat on the streets
Every summer Paris grooves to the beat of African drumming in street parades and music festivals. Different African nations and ethnic groups showcase their own drums and beats.

YOU CAN'T BEAT THIS!

IN THE MIX

Can't even say "mbalax," let alone know what it is? Mbalax is the sounds of Senegal that can be heard on the streets of Paris, along with Amazigh music from Morocco, Congolese rumba, Spanish mestizo, French jazz, American hip-hop, British rock, and Italian opera. Paris is a musical mixing pot!

Small singing sensation

Books have been written and films made about the life of singer Edith Piaf. She suffered hardship as a child but went on to become a national treasure. "Piaf" means sparrow—she was only 4ft 8in (142cm) tall.

Columbia

EDITH PIAF

I LIKE TO CRANK UP THE MUSIC

MEOW!

Musical grind

It used to be more common, but there are still street performers in Paris playing mechanical organs that work by the turn of a crank. They bring animals with them to help attract an audience.

Gifted musician

Of the people in Paris—and all of France—who adored the singer-songwriter Serge Gainsbourg, taxi drivers were among his biggest fans! He took taxis everywhere and would sometimes give them the money to pay for things their families needed.

WANT MORE?

Paris hosts a street music festival (*Fête de la Musique*) every year on June 21.

> BUILD A CASTLE AND GET OVER IT.

> YEAH BUT THERE'S NO SURF.

BEACH ON THE SEINE

No beach? Not a problem! Each summer, sand is dumped along the banks of the River Seine in Paris to create *plages*—beaches. At first people thought it was lame, but now it's massively popular. As well as swimming in a pool suspended over the river, there are classic beach activities like kayaking, volleyball, and sunbaking!

Building the beach

To make the beaches, thousands of tons of sand are brought in by boat and spread over an area that is usually a busy road.

HAVE YOU SEINE MY TROUSERS?

Holiday Seine-side

The beach concept started in 2002 as a treat for families who couldn't afford to go away in the heat of the Paris summer. Now everyone's into it!

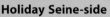

Forget fashion

In some public swimming areas of Paris, boardshorts are banned. Like it or not, guys have to wear tight trunks.

CITY TURNS COUNTRY

It's the busiest road in Paris, but one year it was turned into a field! Just as the banks of the Seine are transformed into beaches each year, French farmers decided in 2010 to clear the traffic from the Champs-Elysées, cover it with grass and plants, and plunk down some sheep and cattle to remind city folk and the government where their food comes from.

WANT MORE?

These urban beaches are open only from July 20 to August 20.

BARON HAUSSMANN'S PLAN

During the 19th century many people left the countryside and moved into Paris to find work. The city wasn't prepared for the numbers of people, and it became overcrowded, dirty, and unhealthy. Emperor Napoléon III decided to do something about it. In 1852, he hired Baron Georges-Eugène Haussmann to give the city a complete makeover. Most of Paris was knocked down and rebuilt, a new road system was laid out, and everything was made to look great!

c. 1850

Before...
Paris hadn't changed much since the Middle Ages. Many areas had narrow, filthy streets and alleys crowded with unsafe buildings that blocked light and air.

THE TIMES ARE CHANGING...

YEAH, PARIS IS GOING OFF!

After...

Haussmann cleared the old city to create a grid of wide boulevards. He divided Paris into districts called *arrondissements* and transformed the sewer system.

Today

Maximum height 66ft (20m)

Roof at 45-degree angle

Continuous balcony on fifth floor

Large stone blocks

Fancy balcony on second floor

A long career

Napoléon III hired Haussmann because he was good at his job, determined, and willing to spend up big. He had 20 years in office before the people of Paris got sick of living with constant building.

THAT HAUSSMANN LIKED A WIDE ROAD!

GOT TO MAKE WAY FOR PROGRESS!

NEW CODE FOR BUILDING

Haussmann didn't stop at redesigning the streets of Paris—he wanted all the buildings to look just right, too. He made many rules about building materials, heights, balconies, and windows that builders had to stick to. Paris soon looked elegant and harmonious. The negative was that rents went up, forcing some people to move to the city outskirts.

WANT MORE?

Make your own city—www.citycreator.com

THE HEART OF ART

The young artists who came to Paris in the late 1800s, determined to make painting their life's work, needed housing and food. So why did they head to Montmartre? What did the hilltop suburb have that other parts of Paris didn't have? It was cheap! Being on the outskirts of the city, it was also not overly concerned with social rules. Here artists could eat, bathe, work, and play as they wished, and follow their passions.

↓ *View of the Butte Montmartre, c. 1830, Louis Jacques Mande*

Montmartre was not only a magnet for painters, but also for sculptors, writers, poets, and musicians.

I DON'T KNOW MUCH ABOUT ART...

The art of saving grapes
Montmartre was once farmland, known for its vineyards and inexpensive wine. The local artists battled property developers and helped to save the last vineyard in town, called Clos Montmartre.

ART MART

The Place du Tertre is the open-air square where artists still paint and sell their work. The square was once free to anyone who chose to set up there. Because of its history and popularity, these days it's run by the government. Artists have to apply for approval and purchase a license to set up here. About 300 licenses are issued at a time.

WANT MORE?

Montmartre official website—www.visitmontmartre.fr

FIGHT TO THE FINISH

So what do you do with an old soldier? Back in the 1600s Louis XIV decided they should be looked after in style. He built Les Invalides, a home for aged French soldiers. They were treated to the best quality food and wine, including large loaves of bread that they could sell or give away. The complex of buildings still houses a hospital and rest home for war veterans.

IF YOU FEEL BAD FOR ME, THINK OF MY HORSE!

I SECOND THAT.

The weight of war
When knights went into battle, killing the enemy was the least of their problems. The hard part was coping with the kind of full-plate steel armor that's on display at the Musée de l'Armée in Les Invalides! It has weapons and military machinery from the Stone Age onward.

MILITARY SECRET

The models of French cities housed in the Musée des Plans-Relief (handmade—there were no computer graphics then!) were hush-hush for security reasons until about 40 years ago. Now we've all been given clearance to view these military models.

Military zone
In the group of buildings that make up Les Invalides, there's a church with the bodies of famous soldiers, a museum that houses to-scale models of cities, and a museum devoted to wars through the ages.

> I LOST A LEG BUT I KEPT MY PRIDE!

WANT MORE?

Les Invalides—www.invalides.org

INDEX

NOT-FOR-PARENTS
PARIS
EVERYTHING YOU EVER WANTED TO KNOW

1st Edition
Published August 2011

Conceived by Weldon Owen in partnership with Lonely Planet
Produced by Weldon Owen Pty Ltd
42–44 Victoria Street, McMahons Point
Sydney NSW 2060, Australia

Copyright © 2011 Weldon Owen Pty Ltd

WELDON OWEN PTY LTD
Managing Director Kay Scarlett
Publisher Corinne Roberts
Creative Director Sue Burk
Senior Vice President,
International Sales Stuart Laurence
Sales Manager, North America Ellen Towell
Administration Manager,
International Sales Kristine Ravn
Managing Editor Averil Moffat
Project Editor Lachlan McLaine
Designer Agnieszka Rozycka
Images Manager Trucie Henderson
Production Director Todd Rechner
Production and Prepress Controller Mike Crowton

Published by
Lonely Planet Publications Pty Ltd ABN 36 005 607 983
90 Maribyrnong St, Footscray, Victoria 3011, Australia

ISBN 978-1-74220-817-6
10 9 8 7 6 5 4
Printed in China

A WELDON OWEN PRODUCTION

Credits and acknowledgments

Key tcl=top center left; tl=top left; tc=top center; tcr=top center right;
tr=top right; cl=center left; c=center; cr=center right; bcl=bottom center
left; bl=bottom left; bc=bottom center; bcr=bottom center right;
br=bottom right; bg=background

10tr, 14cr, 14-15t, 17b, 19br, 21tr, 24tr, 27tr, 35cr, 39br, 41cr, tr, 42tr, 42c, 50,
55bl, 59br, 61tr, 63tr, br, 66r, b, 69c, 75tr, 80-81t, 83br, 85br, 86-87t, 88bg,
90bg, 91bl, 92cl, c, bl **Alamy**; 12c, br, 16r, 47tl, 48b, 52c, 56bl, 69bc, 73b,
74cr, br, 80cr, 82, 83tcr, tr, 85cr, 89bl, 90tc, l c, bl, b, 91cr, 93br **Bridgeman
Art Library**; 31tr **ClipArtOf.com**; 10b, 13cr, tr, b, 14bl, 15br, 16l, 17r, 18l,
19tr, 20l, 21cl, br, 24-25bg, 25t, cr, b, 28cl, 33tl, 34bl, 36l, 37cr, 39tr, c, 43tl,
46br, 51tr, 53c, 55tr, br, 59tr, b, 60cr, 61br, 64-65tl, 67, 69cl, 70br, 71t, tr, c, cl,
76-77c, 80bcl, 86br, 87bl, 93t **Corbis**; 56tr **Flickr/damn_cool**; 6tr, 7tr, br,
8cr, 9cr, 10cr, 13l, 15cl, 24c, 26tr, 28bl, br, 29br, 31cr, 32tr, c, 41bl, 44bl,
44-45t, 45bl, 49b, 50bl, 51cl, 53cl, br, 59t, c, 68bl, 69r, 70tr, 75bl, 76b, 79cl,
87tc **Getty Images**; 15bl **Hachette**; 6b, c, 7tl, 8t, 9cl, 11bg, 17l, 19c,
20-21bg, 22tr, br, 23tcl, cl, tr, cr, b, br, 24bl, 27br, 28cr, c, 33cl, 34cr, 36b,
39cl, 42bl, 44-45cs, 46, 47r, 48tr, bl, 51br, 53tr, 56tl, 57br, 60-61bg, b, t, 62bl,
68-69bg, 70l, 71br, 73br, 74tl, 75tr, 76-77bg, 84tr, bl, 86l, 87t, br, 85c, b, 88b,
89tl, 89bl, 92br, 79b **iStockphoto.com**; 49bl, 61cl, 74bc **Lonely Planet**;
66c **Marcin Wichery**; 15cr **Mary Evans Picture Library**; 31bl **National
Geographic Society**; 7bl, 8bl, b, 9tr, bl, 10cl, 11tl, 16c, 17c, 19cl, bl, b, 20cr,
b, 22bl, tcr, 26cl, 30, 35cl, b, br, 36-37c, 38br, 39tl, bl, 40cr, br, 43t, cr, bl,
45cr, 52bl, 53b, 54bcr, 58b, 62-63tc, 65b, br, 66cr, br, 68c, 68-69tr, 72tl, 74c,
75br, 76c, 79br, 81br, 84tl, br, 85bl, 89tr, 92-93bg **Photolibrary**; 29tr
Photoshot; 12tr, 23tl, 40tbg, 41tl, 47cr, 51br, 54cr, 58t, 64-65sb, 68br, 70bc,
72b, 80bl, 87tr, 90br **Shutterstock**; 60bl, 63t, 77br **Superstock**; 14cl,
43br, 58bl, bc, bcr, br, 59bl, 62-63b, 74tr, 91tr **Vectorstock**; 37tl, 51tl, 57tr,
66tr, 78-79bg **Wikipedia**

All repeated image motifs courtesy of **iStockphoto.com**.

Illustrations

Cover illustrations by Chris Corr

6bl, 26-27c, 29b, 32-33b, 38-39t **Faz Choudury/The Art Agency**; 33br,
40t, 78tl, tr, 79cr **Rob Davis/The Art Agency**; 35t, 47br, 49t, 54l, 65c,
72-73t, 78cl, 80br **Geraint Ford/The Art Agency**; 17t, 42tr, 62-63bg
Aggie Rozycka; 228-29 **Anne Winterbotham**

Maps 44cl, 72cl **Peter Bull Art Studio**

All illustrations and maps copyright 2011 Weldon Owen Pty Ltd.

LONELY PLANET OFFICES

Australia Head Office
Locked Bag 1, Footscray, Victoria 3011
Phone 03 8379 8000 Fax 03 8379 8111
Email talk2us@lonelyplanet.com.au

USA
150 Linden St, Oakland, CA 94607
Phone 510 250 6400 Toll free 800 275 8555 Fax 510 893 8572
Email info@lonelyplanet.com

UK
2nd fl, 186 City Rd, London EC1V 2NT
Phone 020 7106 2100 Fax 020 7106 2101
Email go@lonelyplanet.co.uk